Chicago Burlington & Quincy Railroad Company

Landscape Wonders of the Western World

Chicago Burlington & Quincy Railroad Company

Landscape Wonders of the Western World

ISBN/EAN: 9783337734992

Printed in Europe, USA, Canada, Australia, Japan

Cover: Foto ©Andreas Hilbeck / pixelio.de

More available books at **www.hansebooks.com**

LANDSCAPE WONDERS

WESTERN WORLD.

Landscape Wonders

WESTERN WORLD

―――

COMPLIMENTS OF THE

PASSENGER DEPARTMENT

"BURLINGTON ROUTE"

C., B. & Q. R. R.

―――

CHICAGO, ILLINOIS.

1883.

"BURLINGTON ROUTE," (C., B. & Q. R. R.)
Grand Passenger Station on Canal St., between Madison and Adams Sts.,
CHICAGO, ILL.

INDEX

The Great Burlington Route

Interior View of one of the famous Dining Cars, running only on the C. B. & Q. R. R. Strictly first-class meals only 75 cents.

INTRODUCTORY

T HIS pamphlet has been prepared with a view to impart-
ing such information as must be of interest to any
one contemplating a trip to California, and to that
vast and independent order known as "the traveling public" across the American continent, it is dedicated, with the
compliments of the

Great "Burlington Route."

It contains carefully prepared information concerning all
routes to the Pacific Slope, the sights to be seen on the way, and
the points of interest after one reaches there, and may well
be preserved as a brief but comprehensive budget of information about the whole "far West."

If tourists and travelers generally will take the pains to read
carefully the succeeding pages, they will in a short time gain
valuable insight into many matters which it will be greatly to
their advantage to know, and which they would otherwise
have to pick up at random.

The Great Burlington Route

Interior View of one of the luxurious C. B. & Q. Smoking Cars,
run only by this line for the exclusive use
of first-class passengers.

I.

AROUND THE WORLD.

Hints to European and Pacific Ocean Travelers.

THE time has long gone by when tourists around the world were compelled, for want of better means, to make the entire trip by sea. It was once a wearisome jaunt of months, and sometimes years, with naught but the unvarying monotony of sky and waves to reward the traveler for his pains. But within the past few years, with the improved modes of travel by both land and sea, it has even grown into favor as a pleasure excursion for those who love to rove. For the thousands in Europe and America who have the time and money there can be no more practicable, pleasurable or instruct-ive way of spending a year than this same " trip around the world." The pleasures and advantages of modern trans-con-tinental travel, as contrasted with the tedious, old, all-water route between Europe and Australia or the East Indies, are fast becoming appreciated in both the Old World and the New.

Persons planning a trip around the world, or tourists across the American continent, going either from Europe to Aus-tralia or from Australia to Europe, should read carefully the pages of this pamphlet, select their route and tell the book-ing agent in the port they sail from that they wish to pass through the United States via the Burlington Route. In case

the booking agent can not give a direct order on the Burlington
Route, the tourist should take such order as may be obtainable,
and, on landing in America, if he will present it to the railroad
ticket agent and say that he wishes to cross the continent by
the Burlington Route, a ticket will be given him accordingly.
Travelers may thus save themselves both money and trouble
and have the pleasure of viewing every variety of American
scenery, including the grandest parts of the Rocky Mountains,
the principal cities of the New World and the ruins of the
ancient Aztec civilization.

The different Atlantic steamship lines book passengers
through from London or Liverpool to Australia and Asia with
orders on the American railroad lines in New York. These
orders entitle the bearer to the choice of any line of the Burlington Route across the American continent, and to an allowance of 250 pounds of luggage. Tickets via the Burlington
Route may also be purchased in the principal Atlantic seaboard
cities on the American side. These tickets allow the traveler
several different ways of passing between the Atlantic seaboard
and Chicago, giving him, as his taste may direct, a choice of
scenery, taking in by the more southerly lines the historical
Harper's Ferry and the famous Horseshoe Bend, or by northern
lines the great Niagara Falls. The time between the seaboard
and Chicago is about thirty-six hours, and the trip is made
without change of cars.

Travelers going east from China, India or Australia to
Europe will have no trouble in making close connections at
San Francisco and New York, for trains by the Burlington
Route across the continent leave San Francisco daily, and
steamers for Liverpool and London leave New York every
day but Friday, by one or other of the various lines.

Travelers going west—to Australia, Yokohama, or Hongkong—will do well, however, to time their departures from
Europe, or their tarrying in America, so as to make connections
with the Pacific steamers leaving San Francisco, as per time
tables on the last pages of this pamphlet.

II.

OVERLAND TO THE PACIFIC.

SEVEN WAYS OF CROSSING THE AMERICAN CONTINENT.

THE Chicago, Burlington & Quincy Railroad, "Burlington Route," with its connections, stretches out over the whole western part of the United States, starting at Chicago, Peoria and St. Louis, and, like an immense drag-net, sweeps every part of the West from the eastern edge of the Mississippi Valley to the golden slope of the Pacific.

It thus offers to the tourist no less than seven incomparable routes through the Western World, including every object of interest in that vast domain, from the cold cattle ranges of the North to the sun-mellowed plains of the Mexican border. These seven routes will be described in detail in the succeeding pages, but, in order to give the traveler a bird's-eye view of their attractions, they are here briefly outlined in the beginning.

Route No. 1.

The first route is from Chicago, Peoria or St. Louis, via Galesburg, Burlington, Council Bluffs, Omaha, Fremont, North Platte, Cheyenne, Ogden and Sacramento. (See description of Route on page 17.)

Leave Chicago 12.45 noon, Peoria 4.00 p. m., or St. Louis 8.55
a. m.—dinner for passengers from Chicago on the cars, dinner
for passengers from St. Louis at Beardstown ; Chicago and
Peoria passengers arrive Galesburg 6.55 p. m.—supper on the
cars ; all reach Burlington (an eating station) 8.50 in the evening,
and Red Oak next morning at 7—breakfast in the dining car;
arrive at the Union Pacific transfer at 9.50, arrive at Omaha
9.45 in the morning; dinner at Omaha ; leave Omaha 12.05,
and arrive Grand Island 5.40 p. m.—supper at the station ;
Cheyenne 7.00 next morning — breakfast at the station ;
Rawlins 2.35 p. m.—dinner at the station, supper at Green
River at 7.45 p. m., and breakfast next morning (third day out
from Chicago, Peoria or St. Louis) at 6.00 a. m. at Ogden; arrive
Terrace 12.25 p. m.—dinner : Elko at 7.20 in the evening—
supper ; breakfast next morning at Reno at 7.40, and arrive
at Blue Canon for dinner at 12.45; arrive San Francisco at 8.40
p. m., four days out from Chicago, in ample time to go to a
hotel and prepare for a good supper.

Route No. 2.

The second route is from Chicago and Peoria, to Kansas
City, and thence via Hutchinson, Trinidad, Las Vegas,
Deming, Tucson and Los Angeles, taking in New Mexico,
Arizona and Southern California. (See description of Route
on page 29.)

Leave Chicago 10.00 p. m., or Peoria 9.40 p. m.; leave Quincy
10.30 next morning after breakfast—dinner at Macon ; leave
Macon 2.25 p. m.—supper at Cameron Junction ; leave Cameron Junction 6.30 ; arrive Kansas City 9.05 in the evening ;
leave Kansas City (via Atchison, Topeka & Santa Fe Railroad)
at 10.00 p. m., arrive Newton 7.30 next morning—breakfast ;
arrive Kinsley 1.10 p. m.—dinner ; arrive Coolidge 7.30 p. m.
—supper ; arrive Raton 7.30 a. m. (third morning out from
Chicago or Peoria)—breakfast here ; arrive Las Vegas 1.05
p. m.—dinner ; arrive Wallace 7.10—supper ; arrive Deming
7.00 a. m.—breakfast ; leave Deming, via Southern Pacific, at

7.80 ; arrive Bowie 12.35 P. M.—dinner ; arrive Tucson 6.00 P. M.—supper, fourth evening out ; arrive Yuma next morning at 6.00 o'clock—breakfast; Colton 2.30 P. M.—dinner; Los Angeles 5.15 P. M.—supper ; Merced 8.20 A. M.—breakfast ; San Francisco 2.40 P. M.—sixth day after starting.

Route No. 3.

The third route is from Chicago, or Peoria, via Galesburg, Quincy, Kansas City, Topeka, Ellis and Denver, to Cheyenne, and thence same as Route No. 1. (See description of Route on page 34.)

Leave Chicago 10.00 P. M.; or leave Peoria at 9.40 P. M.; arrive Galesburg 4.13 A. M.; arrive Quincy 8.20 for breakfast ; cross the Mississippi ; arrive at Macon 2.05 P. M. for dinner ; arrive Cameron at 6.15 for supper, and thence to Kansas City, arriving at 9.05 P. M.; leave Kansas City, via Kansas Pacific Division of the Union Pacific, at 9.55 P. M.—breakfast at Brookville at 6.30 A. M.; arrive at Wallace at 3.25 P. M. for dinner ; arrive Hugo at 7.15 P. M. for supper, and arrive Denver at 11.45 P. M. At Denver the train turns northward to Cheyenne, arriving at Cheyenne at 6.00 A. M. for breakfast, and thence westward same as Route No. 1.

Route No. 4.

The fourth route is from Chicago, Peoria or St. Louis, via Burlington, Plattsmouth, Lincoln (Neb.), Hastings, Red Cloud, Denver, Pueblo, Salt Lake City, Ogden and Sacramento, to San Francisco. (See description of Route on pages 17 and 38.)

Leave Chicago at 12.45 noon—dinner in the dining car ; or leave Peoria at 4.00 P. M. and both arrive at Galesburg at 6.55 P. M., in time for supper in the dining car. St. Louis passengers, leaving St. Louis at 8.55 A. M. same day, take dinner at Beardstown, and connect with Chicago and Peoria passengers at Monmouth. All arrive at Burlington, an eating station, at 8.50 (or supper in the dining car); leave Burlington at 9.10 P. M.

reaching Red Oak at 7.00 next morning—breakfast on the cars; arrive Pacific Junction 8.20 A. M., and Lincoln at noon—dinner at the station—supper at 6.20 in the evening at Red Cloud; and reach Denver at 7.30 next morning, in time for breakfast. Or passengers can leave Chicago at 10.00 P. M., Peoria at 9.40 P. M., St. Louis 7.50 P. M.—all arrive at Burlington at 6.30 next morning—breakfast at station; arrive Chariton at noon—dinner in the dining car ; arrive Pacific Junction 6.10 P. M.—supper; arrive Red Cloud 7.00 A. M.—breakfast at the station; arrive McCook noon—dinner at station; arrive Denver 7.25—supper.

Leave Denver at 7.50 P. M.; arrive South Pueblo at 12.25 night; pass through the Grand Cañon of the Arkansas, then through Marshall Pass ; arrive Sargent at 8.05 next morning for breakfast; arriving at Cimarron at 11.25 for dinner; and arrive at Cisco at 6.25 for supper; arrive at Salt Lake City at 6.16 A. M., and leave at 6.26, arriving at Ogden at 6.45 A. M. for breakfast, and proceed thence to San Francisco same as Route No. 1.

Route No. 5.

The fifth route is from Chicago, or Peoria, via Galesburg, Quincy, Cameron Junction, Kansas City, Atchison, Table Rock, Red Cloud to Denver, and thence south to Pueblo, via Route No. 4, or north to Cheyenne via Route No. 3, and thence on to San Francisco via Ogden and Sacramento, same as No. 1. (See description of Route on page 40.)

Leave Chicago at 10.00 P. M., or Peoria at 9.40 P. M., and arrive at Quincy 8.20 A. M.—breakfast; cross the Mississippi, taking dinner at Macon 2.05 P. M., and supper at Cameron 6.15 P. M., arriving at Kansas City 9.05 P. M.; leave Kansas City 9.55 P. M. (again via the Burlington Route); arrive Atchison, Kansas, 11.40 P. M.; arrive at Red Cloud 7.15 A. M.—breakfast; arrive McCook noon—dinner; arriving at Denver 7.25 P. M.—supper. Route from here to San Francisco, via Pueblo, same as Route No. 4, or via Cheyenne, same as Route No. 3.

Route No. 6.

The sixth route is from Chicago, Peoria or St. Louis, via Galesburg, Burlington, Lincoln, Hastings, Red Cloud, Denver, Cheyenne, Ogden and Sacramento. (See description of Route on pages 17, 22 and 27.) From Denver, Route is same as No. 3.

The trip as far as Denver via this route will be the same as by Route No. 4 ; or passengers can leave Chicago at 10.00 P. M., Peoria 9.40 P. M., or St. Louis at 7.50 P. M., and arrive at Denver 7.25 P. M. But from Denver, instead of striking south via Pueblo, as in Route No. 4, the traveler goes north via Cheyenne, same as Route No. 3, and thence west to Ogden and San Francisco, as in No. 1.

Leave Denver at 1.15 A. M., and arrive Cheyenne at 6.00 A. M., for breakfast.

Route No. 7.

The seventh route is from Chicago or Peoria, via Galesburg, Burlington, Hopkins, St. Joseph, Atchison, Topeka, and thence the same as Route No. 2 or No. 5. (See description of Routes 2 and 5, on pages 29 and 40.)

Leave Chicago 10.00 P. M.,˜or Peoria at 9.40 P. M.; arrive Burlington 6.30 A. M.—breakfast; arrive Chariton 11.55 A. M.—dinner; arrive Hopkins 4.50 P. M. ; thence via Kansas City, St. Joseph & Council Bluffs Railroad, arriving at St. Joseph at 7.25—supper ; arrive Atchison 8.40 in the evening ; leave Atchison 10.25 P. M. via Atchison, Topeka & Santa Fe Railroad; arrive Topeka 12.50, after midnight, and there connect with through train from Kansas City and proceed to San Francisco via Route No. 2. Train via Route No. 5 leaves Atchison at 11.40 P. M., and runs via Denver.

The Great Burlington Route

Interior View of one of the celebrated Pullman (sixteen-wheel) Sleeping Cars, running only on the C. B. & Q. R. R.

III.

FARM AND MEADOW LAND.

Pastoral Scenes Along the Main "Burlington Route" to Omaha.

(See Itinerary, Route No. 1, page 11.)

THE journeyer is standing in the magnificent Chicago, Burlington & Quincy Depot, in the city of Chicago. It stretches from Madison street 1,100 feet in length to Adams, and from Canal street to the Chicago river, 300 feet in width. The building is one of the most imposing in the city, and contains elegant waiting rooms, dining rooms, news depots, barber shop and bath rooms, and every possible convenience and comfort for travelers. "All aboard!" cries the conductor, and the tourist steps on board of a train of palace sleeping, parlor and smoking cars, with a magnificent dining car attached, and in a moment is on his way out of the great city. The train in which he finds himself whirling along is as perfect in its appointments as modern ingenuity can devise—one long chain of superb parlor cars, reclining-chair cars, with toilet rooms and porters, easy-chair "smokers," handsome Pullman sleepers and luxurious dining cars—so that the traveler may rest and lounge, or read, smoke, eat, and enjoy the scenery to the fullest measure of his heart's desire and with the least possible ennui from the journey.

Twelve miles through a constant succession of beautiful suburban residences, embowered in shrubbery and flowers, and
Riverside is reached, on the banks of the Desplaines river, up
which Louis Joliet and Father Marquette ascended in 1673
from the village of the Illinois Indians to the lakes.

Through lovely suburban towns and homes, twenty-six miles
farther, and Aurora comes into view. It is picturesquely situated on Fox river, which was also explored by Joliet and Marquette in 1673. The first white man's cabin ever erected in the
county was built on the bank of the river in 1833. Here was the
starting-point of the vast Chicago, Burlington & Quincy Railroad system, with the little thirteen-mile-long "Aurora Branch."
The car and locomotive works at this place employ nearly 1,500
men, whose wages amount to $80,000 a month, and the annual
business aggregates nearly $1,500,000.

Plano, fifteen miles farther on, is the residence of Joseph
Smith, the leader of the anti-polygamous Mormons, and a son
of the old prophet.

Sixty-one miles from Chicago is Somonauk station, near
which the Sac Indians, in 1832, massacred three families of
white settlers — Halls, Davises and Pettigrews — numbering
fifteen persons. Two young girls, Sylvia and Rachel Hall,
were carried off as prisoners, but were afterwards ransomed
through the efforts of a Winnebago chief.

Princeton, forty-five miles onward, was long an important
station on the old State road from Peoria to Galena. It was
settled by colonists from Northampton, Massachusetts, and
until the close of the Black Hawk war, in 1833, was much
harassed by Indians.

Twenty-six miles farther is passed the pretty little village of
Kewanee, the name meaning in the Winnebago tongue "Prairie
Hen."

Galesburg, a hundred and sixty-four miles from Chicago, is
the junction of the main line of the Chicago, Burlington &
Quincy road with its Peoria and Quincy divisions. It is a
prosperous city of nearly 15,000 inhabitants, surrounded by a

splendid farming country. It is the seat of a university, a college and several excellent schools. It has a number of extensive manufacturing establishments, and railroad machine and repair shops.

At Burlington the majestic Mississippi is crossed on a bridge which, with its approaches, is over a mile in length—a master-piece of engineering skill and taste. From the bridge a mag-nificent view is obtained of the river and its green, dot-like islands, and of the beautiful city rising street above street in a grand semicircular amphitheatre of hills. The scenery all around is romantic in the highest degree. The view from North Hill, in the upper part of the city, is a glorious vista of river and island, woodland, field, meadow and rolling hills. Just below the city is Cascade Falls, a dainty little miniature of Minnehaha. The vast rock quarries everywhere around are an almost unbroken mass of crinoids or stone lilies, the most beautiful of fossils.

The whole journey from Chicago to Burlington has been a two-hundred-and-seven-mile-long vista of beauty; a flying pan-orama of prosperous towns and glorious country homes; a whirl-ing vision of the finest farming region on the globe; of handsome houses, surrounded by groves and shrubbery and flowers, wav-ing grain fields, orchards, vineyards and green pastures, be-sprinkled with clover blooms and dotted with sleek herds of thoroughbred cattle. The route through Iowa is much the same, except that the country is more undulating and bears more evidence of newness.

Twenty-eight miles west of Burlington is Mount Pleasant, "the Athens of Iowa," famous for its colleges and schools; and where is found in great abundance a rarely beautiful stone, the star coral, that takes the polish of marble with all the ex-quisite markings of coral.

A rush of forty-seven miles farther west, and Ottumwa comes into view. It is one of the most important cities in Iowa, situated on the Des Moines river, whose rapids furnish water power enough to run a thousand mills and factories. It

has a population of about 12,000, having more than doubled in
ten years.　It is surrounded by extensive coal fields, immense
bodies of valuable timber, and as fine farming lands as ever
plowshare cut furrow in.

On through an ever-varying, beautiful succession of flourishing towns and cities like Albia, Chariton, Creston, Villisca,
Red Oak, Hastings, Glenwood, the seat of the State asylum
for feeble-minded children; through a grand, far-stretching
fairyland of gently rolling prairie and wildwood, rivers, lakes
and brooklets; through cosy farms, with their fertile grain
fields and clustering orchards, neat houses lost in foliage and
flowers, pastures in which the fat cattle and horses stand knee-
deep in clover and grass; and Pacific Junction is reached.
From here the main line of the Chicago, Burlington & Quincy
road goes west by way of Plattsmouth, where the Missouri
river is crossed on one of the grandest bridges that ever spanned
the turbid flood.　This line from Chicago to Denver and thence
to San Francisco, as described in subsequent pages, is the
famous route through "The Heart of the Continent."

Nineteen miles up the river from Pacific Junction, two
hundred and ninety-four miles west of Burlington, and five
hundred and one west of Chicago, our flying palaces-on-wheels
sweep into the immense and stately union depot in the suburbs
of Council Bluffs.　Until 1846, the ground where Council
Bluffs now stands was a Pottawattomie Indian reservation.
About the time of their removal, the Mormons, driven out of
Illinois, halted here on their strange migration westward.

Leaving the union depot at Council Bluffs, the train speeds
across a magnificent iron bridge that spans the swift-rolling,
muddy Missouri, and in a few minutes lands its living cargo in
the depot at Omaha.

There are four cities in the United States that claim with
reason the title of "Magic Cities."　They are Chicago, Illinois;
Denver and Leadville, Colorado ; and Omaha, Nebraska.　On
Saturday, July 21, 1804, the expedition of Lewis and Clarke,
sent out by the administration of President Jefferson to explore

the vast unknown regions of the Northwest, landed at Platts-mouth, twenty miles below where Omaha now stands, and camped for the night.

The present site of Omaha was entered as a homestead or pre-emption claim in 1853 by William D. Brown, who had for two or three years been ferrying the California gold-hunters across the river at this point. Omaha was founded in 1854. Up to that time it had simply been known as the "Lone Tree Ferry." To-day a handsomely-built city of 40,000 inhabitants crowns the magnificent bluffs, which then were in an unknown land. The Missouri river is spanned at Omaha by a magnificent bridge that cost $1,600,000. The situation of the city is strikingly picturesque, with an amphitheatre of lofty bluffs sweeping around behind it in a grand semicircle.

NORTHERN PLAINS AND CAÑONS.

Across the Plains from Omaha to Cheyenne - - Approaching the Cloud-Capped Peaks.

(See Itinerary, Route No. 1, page 11.)

D URING the first day out from Omaha the road traverses vast prairies which the tourist now sees for the first time in something like primitive nakedness and solitude. Settlements and farms are still seen, but, unlike those in the more populous States adjoining the Mississippi, they appear to be swallowed up in the immensity of the interminable levels which roll off to the horizon like the sea. On the left is the Platte river, through whose valley, entered at Elkhorn, the road runs for nearly 400 miles. North Platte is the principal station on this section of the line, and contains a fine hotel, round-house and machine shop belonging to the railway company. Its population is about 2,000, and it boasts of a

brick court house, a brick school and several churches. Not
far beyond North Platte the rich farming lands of Nebraska
are left behind and the railroad enters an immense grazing
country extending to the feet of the Rockies and covered all
the year round with rich grasses. Herds of antelope appear
feeding or bounding away over the verdurous slopes, and
villages of prairie dogs break the sameness of the view. Sidney,
414 miles from Omaha, is the largest town between North
Platte and Cheyenne. It is quite a prosperous place and the
nearest railroad station to the Black Hills, and daily stages run
thence to the famous mining town of Deadwood. At Archer
the tourist gets the first view of the Rocky Mountains, whose
snow-crowned summits look like clouds. Long's Peak, 14,000
feet high, and the Spanish Peaks soon come more plainly into
view, and away to the north the Black Hills are seen crouching
against the horizon. Eight miles from Archer the train runs
into Cheyenne, settled in 1867, and one of the largest towns on
the line, its population being 4,000. It is the junction of the
Denver Pacific Railroad, and contains a fine court house, city
hall, round-house and public buildings. The railroad hotel is
excellent, and the meals well cooked and served.

UTAH'S GARDEN CHARMS.

**The Home of the Mormons—A Veritable Paradise in the
Midst of Mountain Grandeur.**

(See Itinerary, Route No. 1, page 11, and Route No. 6, page 14.)

"PROCEEDING westward from Cheyenne," says one
who made the trip, "we soon crossed the main range
of the Rocky Mountains at Sherman—549 miles from
Omaha, at an elevation of 8,242 feet—and looked down upon
that vast grassy amphitheatre, the Laramie Plains. On a per-
fectly clear day the view from some of the slopes overlooking

this basin is grand beyond description. The hundreds of square miles of pasture lands and arable valleys lie in full view. Through the centre the course of the noble Laramie river is plainly traced by its broad bands of rich, green meadows, its groves of cottonwood, and at frequent intervals its own shining bosom. Twenty-five miles distant the black clouds of smoke of fair Laramie City mingle with the bluest of ether, and by the aid of a good glass, one can trace the rows of brick blocks, the machine shops and rolling mills of the thriving entrepot there built up under the stimulating influence of the Union Pacific Railway. To the west rise the white peaks of the Medicine Bow range. Southward are the clear-cut, sharp-pointed Diamond Peaks. The Black Hills swinging around on the northern side, form with the main range a perfect girdle and shelter. Dark pine forests lie against the horizon almost everywhere."

At Fort Steele, 695 miles from Omaha, the railway for the second time crosses the North Platte. It is here really a "mountain stream," as it sweeps down freshly from the snowy ranges of the south.

Rawlins is the county seat of Carbon county, and the principal outfitting and transfer point for the Snake River settlement, 75 miles south, as well as for the Ferris and Seminole mining districts, 40 miles north. "Slattery" and "Mammoth" are among the principal mines. There are good wagon roads from Rawlins to these districts, one of them passing on northward to the Big Horn region. Soda beds, similar to those near Laramie, are also found within 60 miles of Rawlins to the north. The country adjacent and south into Snake River Valley is well stocked with cattle. Looking out over the desolate expanse of sand and sage brush at Rawlins, Green River and other points the visitor can hardly believe that Wyoming possesses such a wealth of grazing lands as has been credited her

From Granger the Oregon Short Line strikes off toward the northwest. This is one of the most important Railroad connections of the present decade, opening up to civilization some of the richest regions of the earth. Bearing to the northwest, it crosses the southwestern part of Wyoming and southern and central sections of Idaho, and heads directly toward the rich farm lands and immense timber belts of Oregon and Washington Territory. En route it tunnels the Uintah Mountain range near Ham's Fork, Wyoming, and passes through the noted mountain health resort of Soda Springs. At McCammon it joins the Utah & Northern, which comes up from Ogden on the south, and, after its junction with the Oregon Short Line, proceeds north to a junction with the Northern Pacific in Montana. The Oregon Short Line follows the Utah & Northern track for twenty-five miles and diverges again to the west at Pocatello, Idaho. Twenty-eight miles west of there it crosses the Snake river over the American Falls, a cataract of no mean proportions. Westward along the valley of Snake river the track is laid upon an air line to Shoshone—eighty-two miles of railroad as straight as a die, as solid as the rock upon which its ties rest, and nearly as level as the line along the Platte Valley. Shoshone is about twenty miles from the falls of the same name, called the "Niagara of the West." The river pours an immense volume of water over a precipice two hundred feet in height, situated in a remarkable cañon, whose perpendicular walls, rising hundreds of feet above the falls, add a further feature of interest and of wild beauty. Shoshone is also the junction of the Wood River Branch, running off to the north and opening up a rich country. But still proceeding northwestward, the main road of the Oregon Short Line, passing through a country of great natural beauty and wonderful timber development, joins the Northern Pacific at Umatilla, whence it makes connections with Portland, Oregon, Puget Sound, and all points along the Pacific Coast in Oregon, Washington Territory and British Columbia. The mountain scenery of Oregon, along the Columbia river, has scarce its equal anywhere in the world, for its peculiar startling effects. It is the very tragedy of natural grandeur. The richness of the country, too, is considered very great. It was the Hon. William H. Seward who said, in 1869, "sooner or later the world's ship-yards will be located on Puget Sound." Great interest attaches to the country now, for the rapid development it is undergoing at the hands of the Oregon Short Line and the Oregon Land and Navigation Company.

Evanston, 957 miles from Omaha, lies at an altitude of 6,770 feet. It is the last town of importance in Western Wyoming, and is the county seat of Uintah county.

Echo Cañon is entered at Wahsatch, 968 miles from Omaha. The bright red sandstone crags soon greet you on either side, and assume shapes so wonderfully fantastic that you can imagine them almost anything. Plunging through a tunnel, we pass in quick succession "Castle Rock," with its arched doorway, giant pillars and frowning battlements; "Needle Rocks," sharp-pointed and standing out against the sky like a group of old church spires; "Winged Rock," a ledge surmounted with a mass of sandstone which, from our point of view, resembles the wings of some feathered monster; "Steamboat Rock," named from the immense crag jutting out like the prow of a steamer, with the flag of old Ireland (a cedar in its perpetual green) planted firmly and with never fading colors; "Sentinel Rock," rising up grimly and alone, as if to survey the march of progress; and hundreds of others. It is the grandest place in the world for the exercise of the imagination. Think of any form or figure, animate or inanimate, and it will rise up clearly among these splintered, weather-worn, gnarled old rocks of Echo and Weber Cañons, if you give a lively fancy one-half its wonted play. Echo Cañon was well named, for the shrill whistle of our engine and the softer ringing of the bell seem thrown from wall to wall and intermingled with the steady hum and rattle of our wheels, until a wild and almost deafening Babel of sounds rises from the level of the pretty stream to the summits of the awful cliffs. These "Witches," "Cathedrals," "Devil's Punch Bowls," "Pulpit Rocks," "Swallows' Nests," "Girls of the Period," and their thousand mocking reinforcements along the battlements, seem to hurl back the refrain upon our humble heads as only such a miscellaneous array of talent could.

At Echo City—which is located in a perfect little fairy glen —we enter Weber Valley, and find cosy rural homes clustered along one of the most beautiful of all western rivers. From here the Summit County Narrow Gauge Railway leads up Weber Valley to Coalville, seven miles, where some coal mines are being worked. These streams are full of trout, and water-fowl seem especially fond of the surroundings, for we see them on the river as we pass swiftly along. It would be difficult to find a more delightful spot for a few days' sojourn than here. The cañon above, with its queerly-grouped walls from 500 to 800 feet high, and the dozens of side defiles and rocky amphi-theatres, together with the finny beauties in the clear and rushing waters, would furnish room for a week's delightful exploration.

Weber Cañon has its multitude of attractions, as well as Echo. The rocks change in color to a deep gray, and are less extravagantly shaped, as a rule, than those left behind, still often rising to prodigious heights, and narrowing sometimes to the river's edge on either side. The "Devil's Slide," prob-ably the most remarkable rock formation to be found between the oceans, is soon noticed on the left. It consists of two par-allel ledges of granite jutting straight up along the mountain side fourteen feet apart, and at times fifteen feet high. The Thousand-mile Tree—1,000 miles from Omaha—will be noticed near by, with its very distinct label.

Ogden, reached at length, is the western terminus of the Union Pacific, and the first city of note we enter in Utah. It is 1,033 miles from Omaha, thirty-six miles from Salt Lake City, and 4,340 feet above the sea. From here the Central Pacific Rail-way leads westward 882 miles to San Francisco. Ogden river has its exit from a lovely cañon in the Wahsatch mountains just back of town, and empties into the Weber four or five miles below.

CROSSING THE FAMED SIERRAS.

From Utah into California — Nature Sublime — San Francisco at Last.

(See Itinerary, Route No. 1, page 11, and Route No. 6, page 14.)

AFTER leaving Ogden, the train passes two small stations and in twenty-five miles reaches Corinne, the largest Gentile village in Utah. Skirting then on the north shore of the Great Salt Lake, the tourist reaches Promontory Point, the spot where the two companies building the railroad joined their tracks, May 10, 1869, with a silver-trimmed laurel tie, and spikes of silver and gold. Then comes the Great American Desert, a plateau sixty miles long, covered with sapless weeds and inhabited by nothing but lizards and jackass rabbits—a scene as brown and lifeless as Sahara. Passing Humboldt Wells, where there are some springs which have no bottoms, half a mile back from the station, the train after a time reaches Elko, an excellent eating station and the most important station on this part of the line. Then come Winnemucca, Humboldt —a garden spot in the desert—and Wadsworth, where the ascent of the Sierra Nevadas is begun, and the wearying plains are succeeded by mountain slopes, pine trees and rushing torrents. Two engines are soon required to draw the train. At short intervals there are strong wooden snow-sheds to guard the line against snow-slides. At last Reno is reached, 1,622 miles from Omaha. It is a lively town of 2,000 inhabitants, on the Truckee river, five miles from the base of the Sierras. Thirty-four miles farther is Truckee, the first important station in California, handsomely built and perched high up in the mountains. The lovely Donner Lake and Lake Tahoe are only a few miles away by stage. A few miles farther and the train lands at Summit, the highest point on the Central Pacific

road. It is 7,042 feet above sea level, and the scenery around
the station is indescribably beautiful and impressive. From
Summit to Sacramento it is 106 miles, and in that distance the
descent is very swift until the road reaches fifty-six feet above
sea level. The line runs along the edge of precipices 2,000 or
3,000 feet high, and sometimes glides along a ledge cut out of
the mountain sides by men let down in baskets from the cliffs
above. At Cape Horn the view is very imposing. Colfax being passed the train enters Sacramento, the capital of California
—a city of 22,000 inhabitants. It is built on a broad plain on
the east bank of the Sacramento river just south of the mouth
of the American river. Handsome shrubs are in leaf all the
year round. The capitol building is one of the finest in the
Union. From Sacramento to San Francisco the ride lies
through the highly cultivated valleys of the Sacramento; the
train soon dives into Oakland, a city of 35,000 inhabitants, on
the east side of San Francisco Bay. It is a charming spot, a
favorite suburban home of San Franciscans, and much resorted
to for its drives and scenery. San Francisco lies almost opposite
across the bay. The train passes around to Oakland Point,
and from an immense pier running two and one-quarter miles
into the bay a ferry boat carries the passengers and freight the
remaining three miles to San Francisco.

IV.

THE LAND OF THE AZTECS.

Scenes and Incidents of a Trip through New Mexico, Arizona and Southern California.

(See Itinerary, Route No. 2, page 12, and Route No. 7, page 15.)

THE traveler by this great Southern route views an infinite variety of scenes and people, from temperate to almost torrid climes. The first part of the trip need not be described in detail, for something much like it has been pictured in preceding pages. Suffice it to say, that after leaving Chicago, the tourist on the "Burlington Route" finds himself whirling through Illinois farms and fields. He crosses the Mississippi at Quincy, and makes a rush through the magnificent State of Missouri, sighting such busy towns as Palmyra, Macon, Brookfield, Chillicothe and Cameron, and crosses the great Missouri's muddy flood at Kansas City. The run through Kansas presents an uninterrupted view of pastoral beauty, farm and woodland.

After a refreshing sleep the third night out from Chicago we arrive at Raton for breakfast and run gradually upwards to the Raton Pass of the Rocky Mountains, which we reach as the rays of the morning sunlight glint amongst its rugged rocks. The eternally snow-clad "Rockies" stretch away before us, peak after peak, to the northwest. During the morning hours we sight the wonderful Trinidad Mountains.

Noon comes at length and not long thereafter the porter calls out through the car, " Thirty minutes for dinner," and forthwith we are received in culinary state. This is Las Vegas. Five miles northward are the celebrated Las Vegas Hot Springs, with their great hotel, " The Montezuma." It is a big thing, admirably run, and reached by a " stub-train."

But we do not tarry to bathe in the soft medicinal waters, for our train will not wait, and so, settling ourselves in our seats once more, we speed away again, on, on, reaching in time the town of Lamy, whence a branch road shoots off toward Santa Fe. To see Santa Fe one must devote a day. Santa Fe is the oldest recorded town in the United States; the foundation of it is absolutely lost in the mist of ages, for though the Spaniards took a sort of possession of it in 1542, Santa Fe had been a headquarters of the Montezumas for centuries before then. The houses are flat-roofed, mud-covered, and from a distance you can hardly distinguish the town from the surrounding country. They are built of sun-dried brick, precisely as brick were made in the days of Pharaoh. The streets are narrow, the walls dead, and a carriage and two horses, standing crosswise, will block up a whole thoroughfare. The people dress much after the Mexican fashion, especially the women.

But, coming back from our diversion to Santa Fe, let us proceed on through New Mexico toward California. The next important place we strike is the old town of Albuquerque, the junction of the Atlantic and Pacific, a typical Mexican, though fast ·civilizing locality. The bustle of railway life here does not well accord with the old Mexican element, which will probably go under, and a new Albuquerque of American traders, coal miners and railway constructors and contractors take their place ; in fact, the new town of Albuquerque has already made considerable progress. You are now in a new country, and to a great extent among new people. The climate, too, has completely changed. You are in the land of Aztecs and Indians, in the land of cattle and mines. Grasp the change and you will become at once interested, for here is the home of a civilization as old, it is said, as some of the oldest in the Old World.

"The past of Arizona is," to quote the *Arizona Quarterly Illustrated*, "to be read in the numerous and extensive ruins still to be seen on many of the *mesas*, and conical, turret-shaped hills of this lovely, picturesque country. These ruins—some of them once vast temples and places of public assembly, others the castellated residences of mighty chiefs (at once palaces and strongholds), and others, moreover, villages and populous cities with their thousands of inhabitants—almost all seem to belong to times of which we may be said to 'have no other record.'"

The theory generally received with regard to the Aztecs is, that about the beginning of the sixth century the Toltecs, a civilized people, swarmed in large numbers from their native regions somewhere far to the northeast of Mexico, led a semi-nomadic sort of life about 100 years, then seized on Mexico and adjoining regions, did the greater part of the building now lying in ruins, ruled for about 400 years, were then greatly reduced in numbers by famine and pestilence, and finally superseded by more barbarous tribes, who, in their turn, were subdued and superseded by other hordes, viz., the Aztecs, coming, like the Toltecs, from the northward, and, like them also, a civilized people. These Aztecs took advantage of what was left of the Toltec civilization, adding what they thought in accordance with their own ideas, and continued to rule till they were subjugated by the Spaniards.

From Rincon a branch road strikes off to the south and runs for miles along the banks of the famous Rio Grande, to the city of El Paso, and there it connects with the Mexican Central, which takes the tourist down into old Mexico, through a country toward which the world's enterprise and capital have been wonderfully directed these past few years. Among the points of greatest interest upon the line are the city of Chihuahua and the City of Mexico, the capital of this land of the

Montezumas, with its wealth of minerals and unlimited possibilities.

On, on we speed for hundreds of miles, through the strange and varied scenes of New Mexico, twice crossing the mighty Rio Grande We cover a good many miles in one night's slumber during this part of our journey, and as the sun rises in the heavens next morning we reach Deming Junction, 1,197 miles from San Francisco, and 1,149 from Kansas City. All the amusingly horrible stories to thrill the nerves of new arrivals are told of Deming Junction, but we see there nothing to deter anybody from partaking in great comfort of a good hearty breakfast.

Here we leave the Atchison, Topeka & Santa Fe Railroad and find ourselves launched on the Southern Pacific for the rest of the journey. All the morning long, through diversified scenes novel and interesting to Northern and Eastern eyes, we roll along, crossing, not far from Stein's Pass, the border line into Southeastern Arizona. Shortly after noon we dine at Bowie, and during the afternoon Benson Station is reached. From here the rush goes to Tombstone, where some of the best paying mines yet discovered in Arizona are located. The history of this remarkable name is, that the discoverer of mineral when he first arrived, said he thought he could find mineral in the hills south of Benson. " You will find your tombstone," remarked a cattle drover, sneeringly. The prospector persevered, and when he did "strike it rich" and was requested by his admiring followers to name the district, he said . "Oh, it has been named before. I was told I should find my tombstone." And so to this day the place is Tombstone, and, despite its ominous title, a very busy, prosperous and cheerful place it is.

GUAYMAS.

From Benson, a branch line of the Atchison, Topeka & Santa Fe Railroad runs in a southwesterly direction to Guaymas on the Gulf of California, in Sonora, Mexico, a city that is fast coming to the front as an important commercial mart, and which it is claimed will ere long be the rival of San Francisco. The Atchison, Topeka & Santa Fe Railroad Co. are now considering the advisability of establishing a line of steamers to run between Guaymas and Australia, in the interest of their route.

In the evening we take supper at Tucson, four days out from Chicago, and, passing during the night through the southwestern part of Arizona, awake for a six o'clock breakfast at Yuma. From here we cross the Colorado river and enter the Great Colorado Desert—that vast ocean-bed of past ages, 263 feet below sea level, hung all over with a warm and sand-laden atmosphere, and, after dining at Colton, begin to enter the mellow clime of Southern California, the land of fruits and flowers. From Colton a branch road strikes south to the famed Peninsula of Lower California. It runs through the towns of San Jacinto, De Luz, San Luis Rey and Cordeco, showing the traveler a variety of Californian scenery, and terminates in the typical town of San Diego — a spot familiar by name to every reader of American travel. Los Angeles, a spot whose name has been spread abroad through all the earth, we reach for supper as the sun begins to descend the western sky.

Los Angeles and its vicinity is the prettiest and most enjoyable portion of all golden California. If you have a week to spare there you will regret you had not a month. If you have a month you will probably settle and never leave that lovely region again. If you have time take the train for Santa Monica, from Los Angeles—an hour's run through vineyards and orange groves, through peach orchards and gardens—and inhale the life-giving breeze of the Pacific Ocean, on the shores of this miniature Bay of Naples..

Don't come back to the Santa Monica Hotel for awhile. Turn east off the beach, and drive up the old Santa Monica Cañon. There you will see hundreds and even possibly thousands of the young and old of "the Golden State" camped

3

out for the summer, spending pleasantly what they earned easily.

But our train does not linger at Los Angeles, and we go to sleep in a golden summer evening air, speeding northward toward Central California. Waking in the morning we breakfast at Merced, and during the forenoon come to a junction with the Central Pacific road at Lathrop. At 2.20 in the afternoon, five days after leaving Chicago, we roll into San Francisco, ready for the sights and pleasures of the great city.

ALONG THE RAGING KAW.

The Glories of the Midland Route, and the First View of the Rockies.

(See Itinerary, Route No. 3, page 13.)

THE Old and the New—nowhere does the contrast between them more plainly appear than under the great arches of the Kansas City Union Depot, where tourists by the great Burlington Route strike westward over the Kansas Pacific Railway. Within the memory of many of the younger men who now throng her thoroughfares, Kansas City was a straggling little hamlet, fulfilling no other function, commercially, than that of wood market for the river steamboats, or supply market for an occasional wagon train to the Rocky Mountains.

But the tourist can not tarry. The train has moved slowly out from among the evidences of this now great city, has crossed the quiet waters of the Kansas river a short way from where they mingle with those of the muddy Missouri, has sent its benediction of noise and smoke in among the workmen of the Kansas Pacific shops at Armstrong, and is hurrying on through the fields and forests of the "Golden Belt," a zone of country forty miles in width, extending through central Kansas

and Colorado, from the Missouri river to the Rocky Mountains, and traversed throughout by the Kansas Pacific Railway
and its branches.

For a distance of about thirty-five miles west of Kansas City
the train, flying over its solid bed of steel and stone, follows
the Kansas river, by its north bank, only leaving it, here and
there, to find a shorter way along the base of the bordering
bluffs through some green field of growing grain, or across
the smooth surface of some luxuriant pasture land. It is
scarcely more than twenty years since the owners and almost
only inhabitants of this strip of country were Indians, of the
tribe of Delawares. Upon their removal to the Indian Territory
the land was sold to civilized settlers, and has since been
steadily increasing in value and general attractiveness.

Thirty-five miles from Kansas City the first open or prairie
country is reached. This is near the junction of the Leavenworth branch with the main line. Fort Leavenworth lies
three miles from the city, and is reached by a magnificent carriage road along the bluff.

A short distance beyond the junction of the main line and
the Leavenworth branch, on the north side of the line, is the
now famous Bismarck Grove, where for three years during the
summer season have been held some of the largest out-door
meetings which have ever been known in the West.

From the edge of the eastern woods, before reaching
Bismarck, the tourist catches sight of Lawrence, or rather its
crowning glory, the State University of Kansas. Aside from
this, but little of the city can be seen from the car windows. The
train stands still for a few moments at the north side depot, and
while it stands the tourist is reflective. This is Lawrence—
famous because of her eventful history, lovely because of her
present attractions. Mr. Forney speaks of it as "the city of
freedom and martyrdom, of John Brown and James H. Lane,
where the first great struggle for right took place." Above
the beautiful plateau on which it stands rises an eminence
crowned by the Kansas State University.

More fields, farms and villages for a distance of twenty-nine miles—the villages being Williamston, Perryville, Medina, Newman and Grantville—and the tourist is in Topeka, the capital of the State. Here is a city of twelve thousand people, Its streets are broad, its houses well built, its society of a high order, its business interests flourishing.

Seventy-one miles is the distance from Topeka to Junction City. Between these two points there are eleven towns, named, in their order, going westward, as follows : Me-no-ken, Silver Lake, Kingsville, Rossville, St. Mary's, Belvue, Wamego, St. George, Manhattan, Ogden and Fort Riley. These are among the best towns of the Golden Belt, and the country around them is unsurpassed.

Junction City is one hundred and thirty-eight miles from Kansas City. It is the county seat of Davis county, and has about two thousand five hundred inhabitants. The Smoky Hill river, from the west, and the Republican river, from the northwest, here unite their waters to form the Kansas river. There are seven towns between Junction City and Salina, a distance of forty-seven miles—Kansas Falls, Chapman's, Detroit, Abilene, Sand Spring, Solomon and New Cambria—all prosperous places.

The tourist passing over the " Golden Belt " will not fail to notice the large herds of antelope which are almost constantly in view after the train reaches the western counties of the State. Sometimes they appear to the number of hundreds, but more frequently from twenty-five to fifty compose the herd. Startled by the locomotive's rumble, they stop eating, turn their graceful heads toward the thundering train, then whirl and gallop off beyond the hills ; or, quite frequently, challenge the engineer to a trial of speed, and run at a wonderful rate parallel to the train for miles.

Bavaria, Brookville, Rock Spring, Elm Creek, Summit Siding, Fort Harker, Ellsworth, Black Wolf, Wilson and Bunker Hill are the principal villages on the seventy-seven miles of line between Salina and Russell. Bavaria is the centre of a large and flourishing settlement of farmers from the " Western Reserve," who removed to this locality in 1869.

One hundred and fifty-eight miles from Russell, and the tourist reaches Wallace, the last station of importance in Kansas. The stations between Russell and Wallace are Walker, Victoria, Hays, Ellis, Ogallah, Wa-Keeney, Collyer, Buffalo, Grainfield, Grinnell, Carlyle, Monument, Gopher and Sheridan. This is one of the most profoundly interesting parts of the journey westward, and for a very evident reason. Only a few years ago this territory was said to be worthless. Its destiny was problematical. It was declared dry and sandy and absolutely barren. That was the theory of it. The theory was accepted by some; repudiated by others. The repudiators experimented—by which means they found themselves in the right. The wilderness has been made to blossom as the rose.

Leaving Wallace and passing Eagle Tail and Monotony, the State line is crossed four hundred and forty miles west of our point of departure. Little change will be noticed in the physical aspect of the landscape, except, perhaps, that the prairie becomes more rolling. The train sweeps along over the plain. Eagle and Monotony—old Indian crossings of the Sioux, Arapahoes and Cheyennes, chosen on account of the ample supply of water—Arapahoe, Cheyenne Wells and First View are announced in their turn. If the day be clear, the tourist obtains at this point the first view of the Rocky Mountains. Towering against the western sky, more than one hundred and fifty miles away, is Pike's Peak, standing out in this rarified atmosphere with a clearness which deludes the tourist, if it is his first experience, into a belief that he is already in close proximity to the mountains. Henceforth he feels, in the presence of the mighty peaks which disclose themselves one after another, that he has entered another world—a land of un-approachable beauty and grandeur. Less attention will be given to stations as they are passed, though Kit Carson can not fail to remind one of Fremont's favorite follower and guide, from whom the station derived its name. Wild Horse, Aroya,

and Mirage—so named from the optical delusion frequently
observed during the summer months—are small stations, about
ten miles apart. An hour's ride from Hugo the train stops at
Lake, named from a chain of pools, half a mile long, near the
station. River Bend, upon the Big Sandy river; Cedar Point,
from which a fine grove of pines and cedars may be seen;
Godfrey, the location of coal mines which furnish a quality of
fuel sufficiently good for domestic purposes; and Agate, which
takes its name from the large number of moss-agates found in
the vicinity, are all passed in due time, while the mountains
have been unfolding themselves, as if the wand of some necro-
mancer held them in faithful obedience. Peak after peak
appears. The shadowy range takes more definite shape; the
dark rifts in the cañons become visible, and then, in this trans-
parent air, the whole range for two hundred miles bursts full
upon the view. Less and less heed is paid to objects close at
hand as the tourist moves along in sight of this entrancing
panorama. Deer Trail, Byers, Kiowa, Box Elder and Schuyler
pass almost unnoticed; for the mountains aggrandize as they
are approached, and hold the gaze as the beacon-light enchains
the mariner at midnight. The train rolls on over the swelling
bosom of the prairie and soon makes its last stop at Denver,
the unique and beautiful City of the Plains—a city of which
much is to be said in the pages following.

THE SOUTH PLATTE COUNTRY.

From Pacific Junction via Red Cloud to Denver.

(See Itinerary, Route No. 1, page 11, and Route No. 4, page 13.)

THE route from Chicago to Pacific Junction is the same
as Route No. 1. Leaving Pacific Junction, the train
crosses the Missouri river at Plattsmouth, the landing-
point of Lewis and Clarke's romantic exploring expedition
seventy-eight years ago. The bridge and its approaches over

the Missouri at Plattsmouth is nearly two miles long, and is one of the most notable pieces of engineering in the country. At Oreapolis the beautiful Platte river is crossed, and the train flies on through an enchanting succession of waving fields of grain, groves of elms and cottonwoods, and vast natural pastures reaching to the horizon on every side. Tasteful farmhouses and young orchards dot all the landscape with sweet suggestions of home in what scarce twenty years ago was a wilderness almost unbroken. A two hours' run from Oreapolis brings into view the spires and towers of Lincoln, the capital of the State, a beautifully built and prosperous city of 15,000 inhabitants, in the centre of the rich and fertile South Platte country as it is called ; here, too, are also found the salt basins, where salt-making is carried on. Three divisions of the " Burlington Route " centre here, and in the magnificent depot are the offices of the land department of the company, a department which has done more perhaps than any other agency in bringing in settlers and developing the grand resources of the State. The State penitentiary is located just south of the city.

Ninety-seven miles farther, along the divide between the Platte and Republican rivers, through a land of wheat and corn fields, orchards and rich pastures, everywhere watered by pure streams, and beautified by groves of willows, elms. maples and cottonwoods, and dotted with thriving young towns like Crete, Exeter, Fairmount, Grafton and Harvard, brings the pilgrim to Hastings, where one arm of the " Burlington Route " reaches out to Kearney on the Union Pacific and Platte river, and the other to Red Cloud on the Republican. The trip from Red Cloud to Denver is described in the succeeding account of the great Republican Valley.

THE GREAT REPUBLICAN VALLEY.

An Interesting Run from Kansas City, via Red Cloud,
to Denver.

(See Itinerary, Route No. 5, page 14, and Route No. 1, page 17.)

THE line from Kansas City to Denver, via the "Burlington Route," lies farther north than the Kansas Pacific, and takes the tourist through the beautiful cities of Leavenworth, Atchison, Falls City, Table Rock, Wymore, Endicott, and others. Some of these are among the most thriving young towns on the American continent, and many of them possess historic interest. This is the most desirable route between Kansas City and Denver. After a delightful whirl through the cities mentioned, Red Cloud is reached at length, and from here the road lies through the great Republican Valley.

Red Cloud takes its name from the famous Sioux Chief who was born here. It is a flourishing little town of about 1,200 people, on the Burlington air-line from Chicago to Denver. From Red Cloud west, the route for over two hundred miles follows the windings of the great Republican Valley, than which the world contains no more fertile and beautiful body of agricultural and pastoral lands. All the most nutritious grasses grow wild in rank luxuriance, and there are many acres yet untaken and open to all the world. In these vast unclaimed pastures tens of thousands of cattle and sheep find rich pasturage all the year round, without expense to their owners.

The Republican Valley was historic ground generations before the white settler ever planted his feet upon the eastern shores of the United States. In 1541, seventy-nine years before the landing of the Pilgrims on Plymouth Rock, Coronado, the lieutenant of Cortez, set out from Mexico with eight hundred cavalry, to subdue the seven cities of Cibola, that rumor said lay far to the north and were very rich. Near Riverton, on the "Burlington Route," west of Red Cloud, remains of ancient Spanish saddles, stirrups and portions of armor have been found.

Thirteen miles west of Red Cloud is Riverton, in the centre of the "Nebraska Geyser System," a continuation of the great Yellowstone Park geyser bed. These in Nebraska have long been extinct, but the strange looking cones and chimneys, craters and 'scape-pipes still remain as perfect as in the far-back period when they spouted and sputtered as though Beelzebub was making soup of sinners at their deep-down furnace fires.

Near Republican City, twenty-eight miles farther west, amid a wild tangle of geysers and curious cliffs, are found the remains of countless mastodons, mammoths and other extinct races of animals, among them a woolly elephant with long, curling tusks like those of a gigantic boar, the bones showing that the monster must have been nearly twenty feet in height. The whole region abounds with these strange relics of monsters that browsed, when the world was young, amid sky-sweeping groves of sequoias, of which the big trees of California are degenerate descendants.

At Arapahoe, thirty-nine miles on toward sunset, is one of the most remarkable deposits of silicates in the world, left by the geysers of long ago.

Culbertson, fifty-one miles onward, is in the centre of an almost boundless cattle range, where stock by hundreds of thousands of head can be raised at comparatively little expense, grass all the year, abundant water, mild climate, and even salt springs for salting, leaving nothing to be desired. Thousands of square miles are open to any and every comer with his herd of cattle or drove of sheep.

Eight miles west of Culbertson is Massacre Cañon, where, about ten years ago, the Sioux surprised and slaughtered a large number of Pawnees. Skulls and bones of the victims are still to be seen strewn in the wild gulch.

Shortly after crossing the Colorado line near Collinsville is the scene of the bloody battle of Arickaree Fork, between the Indians and United States troops.

On, on, through a region which the Chicago, Burlington & Quincy road has just opened up to civilization and improvement ; through far-reaching vistas of pasture-lands, and here and there a dreary stretch of alkali and sage-brush ; through a region of great possibilities, where everything is as yet new and crude ; on, on, across innumerable little tributaries of the Republican and the Platte, "arroyos" as they call them here, foaming torrents in the rainy season, dry beds of sand at other times, but always yielding water to any one who will dig a few feet for it ; on, till at last the grand Rocky Mountains loom in view, and with a shrill shriek of delight the locomotive rushes into the Queen City of the Rockies—Denver, a municipal miracle, an infant in years, a giant in development.

V.

DENVER.

The Queen City of the Plains.

THE city of Denver lies at an altitude of 5,197 feet, near the western border of the plains, within twelve miles of the Rocky Mountains, the Colorado or Front range of which may be seen for an extent of over 150 miles. The view of Pike's Peak in the southern part of the range and Long's Peak in the north, is indescribably grand. The "Queen City of the Plains" was born of the Pike's Peak gold excitement in 1858-9. In 1860 it was a straggling camp, consisting principally of log cabins and tents. In 1870 it had a population of 4,579 ; in 1880, of 35,719 ; and within the succeeding year, over 600 buildings were erected, and now the population exceeds 60,000. Its streets are regularly and handsomely laid out ; its public and business edifices and its private residences are elegant and substantial ; schools, churches and newspapers abound, and in short, Denver has every sign of thrift, enterprise, wealth and progress. The new Union Depot is one of the finest edifices for railway uses in America, and the magnificent new opera house, which cost $600,000, is another structure which will challenge admiration. It will therefore be seen that the city of Denver is one of the important landmarks in the great trip across the American Continent, and should not be missed

THROUGH COLORADO.

The Grandeurs of Scenery Crossing the Great Continental Divide.

(See Itinerary, Route No. 4, page 13; and Route No. 1, page 11.)

INSEPARABLE from the history of Denver is the history of the Denver & Rio Grande Railroad, which is one of the most stupendous achievements in the science of practical engineering the world has ever seen. While its branches still form a network over all Colorado, the main line has been extended westward over snowy heights, through deep gorges, across plains and up fertile valleys to Ogden and the eastern terminus of the Central Pacific road. From Denver to Pueblo the railway follows the eastern face of the Rocky Mountain range for a distance of 120 miles. Seventy-five miles south of Denver, Colorado Springs is reached, one of the noted health resorts of the West. Five miles to the west, and reached by a branch of the railway, is Manitou.

This Saratoga of the West, as it is called, lies among the foot-hills of the Rocky Mountains, and with its large hotels is already noted as a summer resort of varied attractions. There are several medicinal springs, and the scenic attractions are among the most beautiful in the State. Williams' Cañon, Ute Pass, the Garden of the Gods, Cheyenne Cañon, Pike's Peak Trail, Seven Lakes, Iron Springs, Monument Park, and Seven Falls, are only a few of the many places to which tourists are attracted by the quaint grandeur which they severally possess. From Pike's Peak the plains, rivers, valleys and mountains of the State are displayed at one's feet in all their picturesqueness and sublimity.

Returning to the main line again, the traveler journeys southward to Pueblo. From here a branch of the Denver &

Rio Grande runs southward to El Moro, where there are extensive coke ovens and vast deposits of coal; and to Silverton,
Durango and Santa Fe. Leaving Pueblo, and making straight
for the blue-tinted mountains which appear in the distance,
the main line reaches Cañon City, from which a branch runs
to Rosita and Silver Cliff, and a little beyond plunges boldly
into the Royal Gorge or Grand Cañon of the Arkansas.
When the train first enters the gorge, the steep sides which
shut out all rays of the sun are only moderately high, but
before many minutes elapse they become grander, darker and
taller, and press closer and closer together. Some of the
pinnacles tower two thousand feet above the track; all
around are grim shades, and a solemn stillness only broken
by the roar of the river which rushes along its rocky bed
in foaming masses beside the track. Standing on the iron
bridge which hangs suspended from the sides of the cañon,
and over the river, the roughest man is silenced by the terrible
beauty around him.

Beyond the gorge, and to Salida, the view is less shut in, and
there are visions had of distant, snowy peaks and quiet valleys. At Salida, situated on the left bank of the Arkansas
river, and within a mountain-girded amphitheatre, an extension
of the railway goes to Leadville, while the main line pushes up
the valley to Poncho Springs. Beyond the town the road
climbs a steep grade, and begins to ascend Marshall Pass.
The track doubles time and again on itself. Now the traveler may gaze down the valley he was so lately treading; and
again may look far beyond where Poncho rests to the high
ranges which stand in massive grandeur against the deep blue
sky. Soon, however, one forgets to notice anything beyond
his immediate reach, and is fully occupied in watching the busy
engines mounting the steep grades by which they slowly but
surely gain the summit. Snowy peaks tower above us ; the air
is cold and sharp; there are barren ledges and desolate wastes.
Soon the summit is reached. Emerging from the long snow-
shed, which protects the track from the fierce snows of the

region, the view which is offered the traveler is replete with
grandeur and with beauty.   To the eastward, and separated by
countless summits which press their heads up at us from below,
are the snow-covered, irregular shaped peaks of the Sangre de
Cristo range.   Nearer at hand confusion reigns; deep gulleys,
forests, sparkling streams and isolated mountain tops appear
in every direction, while, overshadowing all, rises Ouray with
its wooded slopes, and gaunt, bare head.   In the west, mellow,
soft, and haze-obscured, lies the county of Gunnison. From
Marshall Pass to Gunnison, the road extends through fresh
forests, and over cultivated meadows, until the mountain-sur-
rounded plateau in which the city stands is reached.   At the
Pacific slope metropolis of Colorado, an arm of the railway follows up the river to Crested Butte, the Pittsburg of the State,
and the main line continues down the Gunnison river to the
gorge which is known from its sombre coloring as the Black
Cañon.

This rock-bound chasm is wilder, more picturesque and
grander than even the cañon we have already encountered.
The cliffs are fully as high, but their sides are broken into nar
row shelves where shrubs, trees and clinging vines have found
a foothold.   In many places miniature cataracts leap from
dizzy heights into the sea-green waters of the river, or, broken
by projecting ledges, reach the bottom of the cañon in silvery
spray.   Half way through the cañon, the Gunnison turns into
a still deeper gorge to the right, and the road continues by the
side of Cimarron creek, which leads to where the cliffs are
more rugged still.

Escaping from the cañon, the road pursues its westward
course under an open sky, until the Wahsatch Mountains of
Utah are reached.   First comes Cedar divide, climbed by steep
grades, and from whose summit an extended view is had of the
Uncompahgre Valley, the river which flows down its centre, and
the San Juan Mountains in the distance. The snow-tipped peaks
of this range form the southern limits of the Uncompahgre
Valley, the rich agricultural section of the old Ute reservation,

and, from whatever point seen, are grand, beautiful, and full of
picturesque sublimity. Montrose is reached after descending
from the divide. From it an extension of the road will soon
be built to Ouray, situated in the very heart of the San Juan
Mountains, and in a region where mineral is found in rich
abundance. Following the Uncompahgre, after leaving Montrose, the road traverses a valley filled with rich farm land to
Delta. Here the Gunnison river is again encountered, and the
road follows it, through its yellow-lined cañon, to Grand Junction, the extreme western city of the State, built at the head
of Grand Valley.

After Grand Junction the railroad enters upon a veritable
desert. Low, treeless, dry and neglected wastes extend before
one for nearly a hundred and fifty miles. And yet the ride is
not devoid of interest. There is a constant fascination in study-
ing the unfamiliar scenes, and later the Sierra La Salle Mountains rise before one in all their beauty of outline. When
nearly abreast of this range, the road passes Thompson's
Springs, where the Indians have drawn rude hieroglyphics on
the sides of a small cañon, and later crosses Green river.
Turning to the northwest, the road approaches the Wahsatch
Mountains. Soon Price river is crossed, a tributary of the
Green, and later Castle Valley is entered. At its extreme end,
and reached after long twistings and turnings among the foot-
hills of the range, stands Castle Gate, leading into the very
heart of the Wahsatch Mountains, and formed by two immense
towers of red sandstone which have a sheer descent of nearly
500 feet, and are severed offshoots from the cliffs behind them.
Once through the narrow way, and climbing the steep grades
of Price River cañon, the road follows first one stream and then
another, and all the while there are unbroken forests, vari-col-
ored rocks, clear waters, green meadows, tangled brush, and
vistas of distant snowy peaks, which render the journey one of
continual pleasure.

At Soldier divide, on the very top of the range, the road
takes its eagle-like plunge down the western slope, and after

emerging from the various gorges encountered, enters Utah Valley, and is almost within sight of Salt Lake City. The view from this side of the range is one of incomparable loveliness. Eastward are the high peaks which the traveler has but just crossed. At one's feet lies Utah basin, and beyond it to the north Salt Lake Valley, girded by high mountains. As far as the eye can see there are rich meadows. Towns nestle in the midst of green groves, the river Jordan is displayed its entire length, and the lake itself, with mountains rising from its very shores, reflects in its clear depth the fleecy clouds, the tree-covered slopes, and the distant peaks of snow. At Bingham Junction branches of the road extend to Alta and Bingham, two important mining towns of the Territory, but the main line continues up the valley and soon reaches the famous Mormon metropolis, Salt Lake City, which is built on the lower slopes of a *mesa* running down from the Wahsatch Mountains toward the shores of the Great Salt Lake. The streets are broad, shaded and planned so as to form large squares, where houses stand in the midst of green lawns and shade trees. It is, of course, peopled mostly by Mormons, and the buildings they have erected, such as the Tabernacle, the unfinished Temple and Brigham Young's home, are places which are always visited.

To Ogden the railway follows the shores of the Great Salt Lake. On the one side of the track the listless waters stretch away to a shadowy distance, and on the other the Wahsatch Mountains rise in irregular, forest-grown masses. Between the range and the water is a sheltered valley under high cultivation. Farms without number follow one another in quick succession, and the fertile fields form a picture of diverse hues. Now the lake is left behind, the mountains grow deeper, higher and more rugged, and suddenly Ogden, situated in a natural amphitheatre, is reached, the tourist boards the cars of the Central Pacific Road, and is carried over the rest of our country to San Francisco and the Pacific Ocean.

YELLOWSTONE NATIONAL PARK.

THAT indescribable mountain-locked gem of all the world !—the "Nation's Pleasure Ground "—will now receive the tributes of admiring thousands who can easily reach it, via the Utah & Northern Division Union Pacific Railway. At Ogden, tourists take cars of this line to Dillon, there connecting with daily stages of the Gillmer, Salisbury & Co. line for Virginia City, Montana, fifty-six miles distant. A good wagon road leads from Virginia City through the most picturesque sections of Montana to the Geysers, a distance of ninety-five miles, and tourists are carried to and from Lower Geyser Basin at low rates. An excellent hotel has been erected at this point where visitors can be made comfortable. The time required from Virginia City to Lower Geyser Basin is about eighteen hours.

The Great Burlington Route

Interior View of one of the elegant C. B. & Q. Parlor Cars, with Reclining Chairs.

VI.

AT THE GOLDEN GATE.

San Francisco — The Queen City of the Far-Famed " Pacific Slope."

WE have at last arrived at the jumping-off place of our great continent, within sight of where the glorious Golden Gate opens out into the limitless expanse of ocean and sunset.

In May, 1850, the city of San Francisco first entered upon its formal and legally recognized existence as an independent municipality. The total land area of the city and county is 26,681 acres ; its average breadth, from bay to ocean, being four and one-half miles by six and one-half miles in length. The peninsula on which the city is located is about thirty miles long by fifteen wide, the city and county occupying the western end. The total value of real and personal property for the year 1882 was $253,000,000. There are 1,100 streets, avenues and alleys, which appear on the map of the city, and 30,000 buildings. There are 113 church organizations. The total value of school property in the city amounts to nearly $1,000,000. It has five first-class theatres and opera houses, four Chinese theatres and twenty-one other proper places of amusement, including Wood-ward's Gardens. It has nineteen academies and places of art ; it has a large number of public buildings, including a United

States Mint ; it has nineteen banks of deposit and thirteen savings banks ; it has the best fire department in the world ; one hundred and ten halls ; twenty-four gardens and parks ; five gymnasiums ; forty-nine hotels, the Palace (the largest in the world), the Baldwin, Occidental, Lick and Grand being first-class ; thirty-eight hospitals ; thirty-three libraries and reading rooms ; forty military organizations and fine military headquarters at the Presidio and at Black Point ; sixty-nine clubs and social societies ; one hundred and sixty-eight newspapers, among which are the daily and weekly Chronicle, Call, Bulletin, Post, Alta, Examiner, Exchange and Report ; seventeen religious and three hundred and sixteen benevolent societies ; seventy-eight protective associations ; five immigration and sixty miscellaneous societies ; twelve street car lines—including five cable roads, which are of great interest to tourists. The population of San Francisco, according to the census of 1880, was 234,116 ; in 1882, about 240,000. The Bay of San Francisco is full of places of interest, conspicuous among which are Alcatraz, Goat and Angel Islands, Black Point, Lime Point, etc., etc. Some of the most attractive places and leading objects of interest in and around San Francisco are the cable roads, Chinese quarters, Golden Gate Park, Russian and Telegraph Hills, Presidio, Cliff House, Woodward's Gardens, Oakland Ferry Building, Safe Deposit and San Francisco Stock Board Buildings, and the handsome residences along the California street cable road.

HACK AND CAB REGULATIONS.—Hacks and cabs are allowed to make the following charges, and any claim for an excess of these rates can be severely dealt with : *Hacks*—One person, not more than one mile, $1.50 ; two or more persons, not more than one mile, $2.50 ; four or less, by the hour, first hour, $3.00, and each subsequent hour, $2.00. *Cabs*—One person, not more than one mile, $1.00 ; two or more persons, by the hour, first hour, $1.50, and each subsequent hour, $1.00.

OFF FOR THE YOSEMITE.

How and When to Get There.

AFTER completing the grand overland trip to San Francisco the tourist will need no urging to visit the wonderful, unapproachable Yosemite. Tourists leave San Francisco on Mondays, Wednesdays and Fridays at 4.00 P. M., reaching Madera, the rail terminus, at 11.45 P. M.; thence the stage ride is divided into two easy drives (ten hours the first day and five hours the second), through one of the most picturesque and pleasing sections of the Sierra Nevadas, and Yosemite reached at noon of the third day. Following are the rates from San Francisco:

SINGLE TRIP.

San Francisco to Yosemite, via Madera $34 00
Lathrop to Yosemite, via Madera........ .... 31 80
Madera to Yosemite.............. .... 25 30

ROUND TRIP.

San Francisco to Yosemite and return...... ....$50 00
Lathrop to Yosemite and return................................... 48 00
Madera to Yosemite and return.................... .. .. 40 00
San Francisco to Los Angeles, Madera, Yosemite and return........ 74 00
San Francisco to Madera, Yosemite, Calaveras Big Trees, Milton
    and San Francisco, or vice versa............................... 64 00
Lathrop to Madera, Yosemite, Calaveras Big Trees, Milton and La-
    throp, or vice versa.... .... 57 00

A writer who once went around the world, exclaimed on his first view of the Yosemite: "My God! self-convicted as a spendthrift in words, the only terms applicable to this spot I have wasted on minor scenes." The pre-eminent grandeur and magnificence of the Yosemite remain untold. Indeed, its charms must really be seen and felt; for it is an absolute fact, that neither pencil nor brush, nor photographic process, can give them faithful portraiture.

Standing upon "Inspiration Point," the tourist obtains the first and most impressive view of the valley, and one that will remain ineffaceably stamped upon his memory. After satisfying the senses with one rapid, general survey of the valley, the eye rests involuntarily upon "El Capitan," the monarch of rocks, and the most matchless piece of masonry in the world; then the vision wanders to the opposite side, and takes in the beautiful waterfall known as the "Bridal Veil;" then the "Cathedral Rock;" then, back again, on the left, to the "Three Brothers;" and, in the distance, the "Dome," "Half Dome," and many other masses of perpendicular granite walls majestically lifting themselves to the sapphire heavens. The valley, which is some six miles in length by less than a mile in average width, is about 4,000 feet above the level of the sea, and is thickly wooded and scattered all over with floral offerings rich and varied, and abundant beyond the gardens of wealth and taste. And, amid the transcendent grandeur of the valley, meanders a stream as cold and as crystal-like as the upper fields of imperishable snow and ice from which it takes its Alpine source. On the crest of the mountains, and at their base, says some writer, and along all the mountain trails, "gush frequent springs for the thirst of the traveler, shooting their sparkling rills across his path as soon as his lips are parched, and inviting him to stoop and drink of a nectar cool with dissolving snows."

THE DASHING OF THE SURF.

Monterey and Santa Cruz — California's Famous Seaside Resorts.

TAKE a tram-car from the hotel to the Townsend street depot, and there buy your railroad ticket to Santa Cruz or Monterey, or, if you have time, you can go to both places—to one from the other. Take your fishing-rod with you on this trip, for mountain trout will be found in nearly every stream you cross.

Monterey and Santa Cruz, situated on either side of Monterey Bay, are fast becoming the most popular seaside resorts of the Pacific Coast. As a winter resort and sanitarium, Monterey has no superior as to situation, climate or accommodation for tourists or invalids. The white, sandy beach, picturesque forests and excellent drives are special features of value to this seaside resort. Adjacent, and convenient of access, are dozens of retired retreats near mineral springs or in charming groves. Single trip tickets, San Francisco to Monterey or Santa Cruz, $3.50; round trip tickets, $6.00; round trip tickets (sold on Saturdays and Sunday mornings, good for return until Monday inclusive), $5.00.

NATURE'S SEETHING CAULDRONS.

A Jaunt to the Famous Geyser Springs — Wild and Wondrous Sights.

THE famous geysers of California are situated about ninety-five miles north of San Francisco, and are reached via two routes—the California Pacific Railroad, via Calistoga, and the San Francisco & North Pacific Coast Railroad, via Cloverdale. The geysers are about twenty-seven miles from Calistoga and fifteen miles from Cloverdale, and are reached by stage from both points. White Sulphur Springs is situated two miles from St. Helena, on the California Pacific Railroad. The Petrified Forest is situated five miles west of Calistoga, at the terminus of the California Pacific Railroad. Low excursion rates are made to parties desiring to visit these places.

THE TRIP UP THE CAÑON.

The first object of interest after passing through the gate ("To the Geysers") is the "Iron Spring," the waters of which are cold and possess curative powers.   You then cross the river, and "Eye Water Spring" meets you, with its colored liquid. You next cross "Geyser Creek," and soon after ascend the steaming, sulphurous gorge and come upon "Proserpine's Grotto," the "Devil's Arm-Chair," "Devil's Kitchen," and "Devil's Inkstand." You then pass the "Hot Alum Spring," and soon after come upon "Pluto's Punch Bowl," the contents of which no one but a salamander would touch, and the very opposite of those ineffable midnight decoctions compounded by some pleasant companion.   Then follow, in rapid succession, the "Geyser Smokestack," "Cold Alum Spring," and then the "Witches' Cauldron," (the most appropriately-named object in the cañon, and a wonder among wonders,) with its black, bubbling waters, 195° Fahrenheit, and of unfathomable depth.   Farther on are the "Devil's Canopy," "Geyser Safety Valve," "Devil's Pulpit," "Steamboat Spring," "Temperance Spring," "Lover's Retreat," "Lover's Leap," "Lava Beds," "Indian Sweat Bath," "Devil's Tea Kettle," "Hot Acid Spring," "Lemonade Spring," "Devil's Oven," and many other objects of this California Hecla.   The round trip is a little over a mile, and takes from an hour to an hour and a half.

THE GIANT TREES.

Vivid Description of California's World-Renowned Vegetable Wonders.

THE Calaveras Grove of Big Trees was the first one discovered by white men, and the date was the spring of 1852.   The person who first stumbled on these vegetable monsters was Mr. A. T. Dowd, a hunter employed by the Union Water Company to supply the men in their employ with fresh meat.   According to the accounts, the discoverer found that his story gained so little credence among the workmen that he was obliged to resort to a ruse to get them to go where the trees were.

The genus was named in honor of Sequoia, or Sequoyah, a Cherokee Indian of mixed blood, better known by his English name of George Guess, who is supposed to have been born about 1770 and who lived in Wills Valley in the extreme northeastern corner of Alabama among the Cherokees. He became known to the world by his invention of an alphabet and written language of his tribe.

The Calaveras Grove is situated in the county of that name, about sixteen miles from Murphy's Camp, and near the Stanislaus river. It is on, or near, the road crossing the Sierra by the Silver Mountain Pass. This being the first grove of Big Trees discovered, and the most accessible, it has come more into notice and been much more visited than any of the others; indeed, this and the Mariposa Grove are the only ones which have become a resort for travelers. The Calaveras Grove has also the great advantage over the others, that a good hotel is kept there, and that it is accessible on wheels, all the others being at a greater or less distance from any road. This grove occupies a belt 3,200 feet long by 700 feet broad, extending in a northwest and southeast direction, in a depression between two slopes, through which meanders a small brook which dries up in the summer. There are between ninety and one hundred trees in the grove, some of them thirty feet thick and three hundred feet high.

The Mariposa Grove is situated about sixteen miles directly south of the Lower Hotel in the Yosemite Valley, between three and four miles southeast of Clark's Ranch, and at an elevation of about 2,500 feet above the last-named place, or of 6,500 feet above the sea level.

The "Big Trees" may be included in the stage ride to the Yosemite Valley.

The Great Burlington Route

Interior View of one of the world-renowned State-Room Cars,
run only on the C. B. & Q. R. R.

VII.

IN GENERAL.

Showing how the "Burlington Route" reaches all Important Points in the West, Southwest and Northwest, in addition to its being the Great Highway for Trans-Continental Travel.

WHILE the "Burlington Route" is the principal line across the American Continent, it must not be forgotten that it is the Great Highway for land seekers, merchants and business men generally, to reach any and all of the important cities in the West, Northwest and Southwest, with speed, safety and comfort. Its system of through cars, and the connections it makes in Union Depots, justly entitle it to the patronage it receives.

Call the roll of great western cities, Chicago, St. Louis, Kansas City, Peoria, Burlington, Quincy, St. Joseph, Rock Island, Keokuk, Davenport, Ottumwa, Des Moines, Atchison, Council Bluffs, Omaha, Lincoln and Denver. All here, and all on the lines of the Briareus-handed, hundred-armed Chicago, Burlington & Quincy Railroad. Ask for all the richest regions in the six grandest States of the American Great West; and they all respond: Here, along the lines of the Chicago, Burlington & Quincy. Inquire for the most glorious health and pleasure resorts upon the globe; and the answer is: In Colorado, at the western end of the Chicago, Burlington & Quincy.

To the traveler on business or for pleasure, going from the East to the West, it is the only through line. To the journeyer from the great lakesides to the Rocky Mountains, it is the only line, direct, owning its road clear through, and running its own cars. From Chicago to Denver, it is the first and only through line, and by many miles shorter than any of the broken and disjointed competing routes. To the grand scenery and health-giving air and medicated waters of the Rocky Mountain Wonderland, it is the only direct route under one management. To the Eastern seeker for a home and a bonanza fortune, it affords the shortest, quickest, cheapest and best route to the broad valleys and prairies, the free pastures and grain-fields, and the daily developing mines of the marvelous Far West. To the Eastern and Southern summer tourist and refugee from torrid heats and lowland miasmas, it presents the most direct and luxuriously appointed highway to all the glorious loitering-places of the American Alps, where snow-capped peaks are ever in sight ; where every breath is full of vigor ; where the eye and heart may feast on all that is most sublime and magnificent in mountain, valley, lake, river, cataract, crag and cañon. The Chicago, Burlington & Quincy Railroad offers every inducement and accommodation. It is the business man's route between the East and West." It is the artist's and tourist's route to all that is most gorgeous in scenery on the continent. It is the homeseeker's route to millions on millions of acres of free farming and grazing lands. It is the stock-raiser's route to cattle ranges and sheep pastures. It is the fortune-hunter's route to all the bonanza mines, present and to come. It is the invalid's route to the world's most glorious sanitarium.

For special information relating to the "Burlington Route," call upon or address,

T. J. POTTER,
Vice-Pres't and Gen'l Manager, Chicago.

PERCEVAL LOWELL,
General Passenger Agent, Chicago.

W. H. FIRTH,
Chief of Traveling Agents' Service, Chicago.

JNO. Q. A. BEAN,
General Eastern Agent, 317 Broadway, N. Y.,
and 306 Washington Street, Boston.

The following Traveling and Passenger Agents of our roads are constantly traveling throughout the country, looking after the interests of our lines, and will at any time call upon parties contemplating a trip to the West, Northwest or Southwest, and, in addition to securing them the very lowest rates of fare, will cheerfully furnish, free of charge, valuable information as to Routes and Connections.

They are supplied with Maps, Time Tables, Guides, and advertising matter of interest to travelers, which they will forward free on application. Their addresses are as follows:

W. C. LOCHERTY, Passenger Agent, 317 Broadway, New York.

W. L. GREENE, Traveling Agent, 306 Washington Street, Boston.

F. WETHERALD, Traveling Agent, Schenectady, N. Y.

J. W. PICKLE, Traveling Agent, 612 Penn. Ave., Washington, D. C.

J. SIMPSON, Traveling Agent, 28 East Front Street, Toronto, Ont.

ROBERT M. SMITH, Traveling Agent, Columbus, Ohio.

T. W. LEE, Traveling Agent, Indianapolis, Indiana.

W. D. SANBORN, Div. Passenger Agent, 112 North 4th St., St. Louis, Mo.

C. E. OSBORN, Traveling Agent, Chattanooga, Tenn.

A. G. SHEARMAN, Traveling Agent, Union Depot, Cleveland, Ohio.

O. WARNER, Traveling Agent, Chicago, Ill.

J. A. QUINLAN, Traveling Agent, Chicago, Ill.

NAT. BROWN, Traveling Agent, Burlington, Ia.

JAMES WALLACE, Passenger Agent, 59 Clark Street, Chicago, Ill.

P. G. BEAM, General Agent "Burlington Route," 32 Montgomery Street, San Francisco, Cal

T. D. McKAY, General Agent H. & St. Jo. and C., B. & Q. Railroads, 32 Montgomery Street, San Francisco.

PARTIES IN EUROPE

Desiring Information about the

"BURLINGTON ROUTE,"

C., B. & Q. R. R. CO. OF AMERICA,

Can obtain the same at any of the following Offices of

Thos. Cook & Son.

CHIEF OFFICE:
Ludgate Circus, London, E. C.

BRANCH OFFICES·

LONDON
- West End Office, 35 Piccadilly.
- Strand Office. 445 West Strand.
- Euston Rd. Office, Front of St. Pancras Station.
- Crystal Palace, Tourist Court.

LIVERPOOL—11 Ranelagh Street.
GLASGOW—165 Buchanan Street.
EDINBURGH—9 Princes Street.
DUBLIN—45 Dame Street.
BRADFORD—8 Exchange, Market Street.
LEEDS—1 Royal Exchange.
SHEFFIELD—Change Alley Corner.
NOTTINGHAM—16 Clumber Street.
MANCHESTER—61 Market Street.
BIRMINGHAM—Stephenson Place.
WALSALL—Postoffice Buildings, The Bridge.
WOLVERHAMPTON—27 Queen Street.
LEICESTER—5½ Gallowtree Gate.

PARIS
- 9 Rue Scribe.
- Grand Hotel (Court Yard).

BRUSSELS—22 Gallerie du Roi, Galleries St. Hubert.
COLOGNE—40 Domhof.
NICE—15 Quai Massena.
GENEVA—90 Rue du Rhone.
ROME—1B Piazza di Spagna.
NAPLES—Sommer's Art Gallery, Largo Vittoria.
MALTA—280 Strada Reale, Valetta.
ALGIERS—Mr. D. Bankhardt.
CAIRO (EGYPT)—Cook's Pavillion.
ALEXANDRIA—Hotel Abbat.
JAFFA (PALESTINE)—Jerusalem Hotel.
JERUSALEM—Outside Jaffa Gate.
BEYROUT—Near Hotel Belle Vue.
CALCUTTA—Northbrook House.
BOMBAY—Hornby Row.

A. R. GREGORY, JR.,
Passenger Agent of the "Burlington Route,"
SYDNEY, N. S. W. AUSTRALIA.

Pacific Mail Steamship Co.

CHINA AND JAPAN LINE.

Miles.	PASSAGE RATES AS FOLLOWS, subject to change :	Cabin.	European Steerage.	Chinese Steerage.
4,800	Between San Francisco and Yokohama....	$250 00	$ 85 00	$51 00
6,400	" " " " Hongkong.....	300 00	100 00	51 00
5,100	" " " " Hiogo..........	268 00	98 00	58 00
5,550	" " " " Nagasaki......	285 00	111 00	63 50
6,000	" " " " Shanghai......	305 00	125 00	71 00

Children under 12 years of age, one-half rates; under 5 years, one-quarter rates; under 1 year, free.

Servants accompanying their employers will be charged two-thirds of cabin rate, without regard to age or sex, and will be berthed and served with meals according to ship's regulations.

250 lbs. baggage allowed each adult first-class or cabin passenger; 167 lbs. each servant; 150 lbs. each European steerage; 100 lbs. each Chinese steerage; proportionate to children. Excess baggage charged for at ten (10) cents per lb.

☞**Round-trip Tickets** between San Francisco and Yokohama or Hongkong, good for twelve months, will be sold at a reduction of 12½ per cent. from regular rates.

An allowance of 20 per cent. on return passage will be made to passengers paying full fare from San Francisco to Yokohama or Hongkong, or *vice versa*, who re-embark within six months from date of landing, and an allowance of 10 per cent. to those who return within twelve months.

Round-trip Tickets from San Francisco to Yokohama and return, good for three months from date of arrival at Yokohama, $350.

To Families paying for 4 full fares, an allowance of 7 per cent. will be made on cabin rates between San Francisco and Yokohama or Hongkong.

Exclusive use of staterooms can be secured by the payment of half rate for extra berths.

WILLIAMS, DIMOND & CO., General Agents,

Office, First and Brannan Sts.,

SAN FRANCISCO.

AUSTRALIAN, NEW ZEALAND
—AND—
HAWAIIAN LINE.

STEAMERS LEAVE PIER, FIRST AND BRANNAN STREETS, SAN FRANCISCO,
At 2 o'clock, P. M.,
Saturday, JUNE 2d, and every FOURTH SATURDAY thereafter, (or
immediately on arrival of the English Mails,) for

Honolulu, Auckland and Sydney,
Connecting with Steamers for
Wellington, Port Chalmers, Melbourne, Adelaide and other Ports.

CITY OF NEW YORK....................June 2,   September 22.
ZELANDIA .. ..June 30,   October 20.
CITY OF SYDNEY ....July 28.
AUSTRALIA ....August 25.

RATES OF FARE.
(American Gold.)

Miles.	SAN FRANCISCO —TO—	CABIN.		Servants.	Steerage.
		Main Saloon.	Upper Deck.		
2,100	HONOLULU	$ 75.00	$10 and $20 additional according to location.	$ 50.00	$ 30.00
6,050	AUCKLAND........	200.00		133.33	100.00
6,625	WELLINGTON	222.00		147.33	114.00
6,795	LYTTLETON..........	228.00		151.33	118.00
7,000	PORT CHALMERS....	232.00		153.33	120 00
7,200	SYDNEY.............	200.00		133.33	100.00
7,740	MELBOURNE.........	212.50		145.83	106.25
7,650	BRISBANE............	220.00		153.33	110.00
7,500	ROCKHAMPTON......	232.00		165 20	114.38
7,600	HOBART TOWN	226.25		159.58	115.00

Children between five and 12 years. half fare; between two and five years,
quarter fare; under two years, free. Two hundred and fifty pounds baggage
allowed each full Cabin passenger; one hundred and fifty pounds each
Steerage passenger; proportionate to Children. Extra baggage, 10 cents
per pound.
Servants accompanying their employers will be charged as per tariff
without regard to age or sex, and will be berthed and served with meals
according to ship's regulations.

ROUND TRIP TICKETS

Will be sold at a reduction of 10 per cent. from regular rates. Exclusive
use of state room can be secured by the payment of half rate for extra
berths.

(64)

PACIFIC MAIL STEAMSHIP CO.

Central American and Mexican Lines.

Carrying Mails of the United States and of Colombia, Costa
Rica, Nicaragua. Honduras, San Salvador,
Guatemala and Mexico.

LOCAL RATES. PAYABLE IN UNITED STATES GOLD COIN.

Miles.	SAN FRANCISCO TO	Cabin.	Steerage.
1,194	Mazatlan	$ 75 00	$ 30 00
1,519	San Blas	85 00	35 00
1,685	Manzanillo	85 00	42 50
1,836	Acapulco	100 00	50 00
2,043	Port Angel	100 00	50 00
2,124	Salina Cruz	100 00	50 00
2,204	Tonala	100 00	50 00
2,306	San Benito	100 00	50 00
2,349	Champerico	115 00	57 50
2,425	San Jose de Guatemala	115 00	57 50
2,485	Acajutla	115 00	57 50
2,523	La Libertad	115 00	57 50
2,627	La Union	125 00	62 50
2,648	Amapala	125 00	62 50
2,711	Corinta	125 00	62 50
2,817	San Juan Del Sur	125 00	62 50
2,973	Punta Arenas	125 00	62 50
3,427	Panama	125 00	62 50

Miles.	PANAMA TO	Cabin.	Steerage.
454	Punta Arenas	$ 40 00	$ 20 00
610	San Juan Del Sur	60 00	30 00
716	Corinta	65 00	32 50
779	Amapala	70 00	35 00
800	La Union	70 00	35 00
904	La Libertad	75 00	37 50
942	Acajutla	80 00	40 00
1,002	San Jose de Guatemala	85 00	42 50
1,078	Champerico	90 00	45 00
1,121	San Benito	90 00	45 00
1,223	Tonala	95 00	47 50
1,303	Salina Cruz	95 00	47 50
1,384	Port Angel	100 00	50 00
1,591	Acapulco	100 00	50 00
1,742	Manzanillo	110 00	55 00
1,908	San Blas	125 00	62 50
2,033	Mazatlan	125 00	62 00
3,427	San Francisco	125 00	62 50

Children under twelve years, half fare; under six years, quarter fare;
under two years, free. Servants accompanying their employers will be
charged two-thirds of Cabin rates, and will be bertbed and served with
meals according to ship's regulations.

Two hundred pounds baggage allowed each Cabin passenger; one hundred pounds Steerage; proportionate to Children. Excess baggage, 5 cents
per pound.

PACIFIC MAIL STEAMSHIP

COMPANY.

CHINA AND JAPAN LINE.

The Steamers of this Line are appointed to Sail
as follows:

STEAMERS.	1883. FROM SAN FRANCISCO.	1883. FROM YOKOHAMA.	1883. FROM HONGKONG.
City of Peking........	March...29	May 5	May 15
City of Rio de Janeiro.	May 17	June....25	July 5
City of Tokio........	" ...31	July 10	" 20
City of Peking.......	June....14	" 24	August.. 3
City of Rio de Janeiro.	August.. 4	Sept.....12	Sept. ...22
City of Tokio........	" ..18	" 26	Oct..... 6
City of Peking.......	Sept. ... 1	Oct. 10	" 20
City of Rio de Janeiro.	Oct. 24	Dec..... 3	Dec.....13
City of Tokio.......	Nov..... 7	" 17	" 27
			1884.
City of Peking.......	" ...20	" 31	Jan. 10

These Steamers are first-class in every
particular, and have spacious and most comfortable accommodations for passengers.

UPB

PACIFIC MAIL STEAMSHIP CO.

PANAMA LINE.

Steamers Leave Pier, First and Brannan Streets, San Francisco,

—— FOR ——

NEW YORK, via PANAMA

On the 1st and 15th of every month, at 10 a. m.

The **Steamer of the 1st** will take freight and passengers for MA-ZATLAN, ACAPULCO, CHAMPERICO, SAN JOSE DE GUATEMALA, ACAJUTLA, LA LIBERTAD and PUNTA ARENAS.

The **Steamer of the 15th** will take freight and passengers for MAZATLAN, SAN BLAS, MANZANILLO and ACAPULCO, and via Acapulco for lower Mexican and Central American Ports, calling at SAN JOSE DE GUATEMALA and LA LIBERTAD, to land passengers and mails.

Each Steamer will take passengers for South American, European and West Indian ports. Through Tickets at Lowest Rates for sale at this office.

RATES OF FARE.

To New York, Cabin, $136; Steerage, $70.

Children between 6 and 12 years, half fare; between 2 and 6 years, quarter fare; under 2, free.

Servants accompanying their employers will be charged two-thirds of Cabin rates, without regard to age or sex, and will be berthed and served with meals according to ship's regulations. These rates include railroad fare across the Isthmus of Panama.

200 lbs. of baggage are allowed to each Cabin Passenger.
150 "   "   "   "   "   " Steerage Passenger.

Proportionate allowance to Children.

Excess Baggage 10 cents per pound. Merchandise, Bedding. etc., will not be taken as baggage; when carried as freight, will be charged 5 cents per pound, prepaid.

For Freight or Passage apply at the office, corner FIRST AND BRANNAN STREETS.

WILLIAMS, DIMOND & CO.,

General Agents.

(67)

1883. TIME TABLE 1883.

—)SUBJECT TO CHANGE.(—

OUTWARD ROUTE.

LEAVE	ARRIVE		
SAN FRANCISCO	HONOLULU	AUCKLAND	SYDNEY
SATURDAY	SUNDAY	MONDAY	SATURDAY
January 13	January..... .21	February 5	February 10
February.... .16	February......18	March 5	March 10
March 10	March 18	April.......... 2	April........... 7
April...... ..7	April..........15	April..........30	May........... 5
May 5	May............13	May 28	June 2
June 2	June 10	June..........25	June 30
June 30	July 8	July...........23	July..........28
July.. 28	August 5	August 20	August.........25
August 25	September... 2	September....17	September .. .22
September.....22	September...30	October.......15	October...... 20
October....... 20	October.......28	November . .12	November.....17

HOMEWARD ROUTE.

LEAVE		ARRIVE	
SYDNEY	AUCKLAND	HONOLULU	SAN FRANCISCO
THURSDAY	TUESDAY	TUESDAY	WEDNESDAY
1883	**1883**	**1883**	**1883**
January.......25	January 2	January.......16	January........24
February ... .22	January......30	February 13	February 21
March 22	February.....27	March 13	March.. 21
April............19	March 27	April..........10	April...........18
May............17	April 24	May........... 8	May...........16
June 14	May 22	June.......... 5	June 13
July...........12	June 19	July 3	July...........11
August........ 9	July...........17	July...........31	August........ 8
September.... 6	August........14	August........28	September.... 5
October........ 4	September ... 11	September....25	October........ 3
November..... 1	October........ 9	October.......23	October........31
	November.. . 6	November....20	November. ...28

OCCIDENTAL AND ORIENTAL STEAMSHIP COMPANY

April. PASSAGE RATES AS FOLLOWS, SUBJECT TO CHANGE : 1883.

(Payable in U. S. Gold Coin from San Francisco.)	* First Class, or Cabin.	European Steerage.	Chinese Steerage.	Distances from San Francisco.
Between San Francisco and Yokohama, Japan	$250 00	$ 85 00	$51 00	4,800 miles.
" " Hongkong, China.....	300 00	100 00	51 00	6,400 "
" " Hiogo, Japan	268 00	98 00	58 00	5,100 "
" " Nagasaki, Japan.....	285 00	111 00	63 50	5,550 "
" " Shanghae, China.....	305 00	125 00	71 00	6,000 "
From " Singapore, India.....	380 00	.....	.....	7,850 "
" " Penang, "	400 00	.....	.....	8,250 "
" " Calcutta, "	450 00	.....	.....	9,900 "

Children under 12 years of age, one-half rates; under 5 years, one-quarter rates; under 1 year, free.

Servants accompanying their employers will be charged two-thirds of cabin rate, without regard to age or sex, and will be berthed and served with meals according to ship's regulations.

250 lbs. baggage allowed each adult first-class or cabin passenger; 167 lbs. each servant; 150 lbs. each European steerage; 100 lbs. each Chinese steerage; proportionate to children. Excess baggage charged for at ten (10) cents per lb.

☞ **Round-trip Tickets between San Francisco and Yokohama or Hongkong**, good for twelve months, will be sold at a reduction of 12½ per cent. from regular rates.

An allowance of 20 per cent. on return passage will be made to passengers paying full fare from San Francisco to Yokohama or Hongkong, or vice versa, who re-embark within six months from date of landing, and an allowance of 10 per cent. to those who return within twelve months.

* *Round-trip Tickets* from San Francisco to Yokohama and return, good for three months from date of arrival at Yokohama, $350.

To Families paying for 4 full fares, an allowance of 7 per cent. will be made on cabin rates between San Francisco and Yokohama or Hongkong.

Exclusive use of staterooms can be secured by the payment of half rate for extra berths.

THE ALASKA ROUTE.

The Steamship IDAHO, carrying the U. S. Mails, sails from Portland, Oregon, on or about the **30th of Every Month**, for Port Townsend, W. T., Victoria and Nanaimo, B. C., Fort Wrangle, Sitka and Harrisburg, Alaska, connecting at Port Townsend with the last Steamer of the same month sailing from San Francisco for Victoria and Puget Sound as per advertisement herein. Passengers at San Francisco for Alaska should take the above named steamers on the Victoria and Puget Sound Route, and Freight should be taken to Spear Street Wharf, from which a Steamer will sail on or about the 30th of every month. It has for some time been the impression among thinking people that really the Government did not pay $7,200,000 for Alaska for nothing. Its grand resources are slowly but surely coming to the front. Visitors go there and come back delighted with the attractions, surprised at its climate, and anxious to return.

VICTORIA and PUGET SOUND ROUTE.

The Steamers Dakota and Geo. W. Elder, carrying Her Britannic Majesty's Mails, sail from Broadway Wharf, San Francisco, at 2 P. M., on

10th, 20th and 30th of Each Month,

For Victoria B. C., Port Townsend, Seattle, Tacoma, Steilacoom and Olympia, making close connections with Steamboats, etc., for Skagit River and Cassiar Mines, Nanaimo, New Westminister, Yale, Sitka, and all other important points.

Returning. leave Seattle and Port Townsend P. M., on the 9th, 19th and 29th of each month, and Victoria (Esquimalt), at 11 A. M., on the 10th, 20th and 30th of each month.

NOTE.—When Sunday falls on the 10th, 20th or 30th, steamers sail from San Francisco one day earlier, and from Sound Ports and Victoria one day later than stated above.

The Steamer Victoria sails from San Francisco for New Westminister and Nanaimo about every two weeks, as per advertisements in the San Francisco *Alta* or *Guide*.

PORTLAND, OREGON ROUTE.

The Oregon Railway and Navigation Company and the Pacific Coast Steamship Company will dispatch from Spear Street Wharf, San Francisco, one of their Steamships,

QUEEN OF THE PACIFIC,
STATE OF CALIFORNIA, OREGON, OR COLUMBIA,

Carrying the U. S. Mails and Wells, Fargo & Co's Express, on

March 31, April 3, 6, 9, 12, 15, 18, 21, 24, 27, 30,

And every three days thereafter, at 10 a. m., for Portland and Astoria, Oregon.

Returning, leave Portland, Oregon, on

April 2, 5, 8, 11, 14, 17, 20, 23, 26, 29,

and every three days thereafter.

Steamer taking combustibles sails from San Francisco about every two weeks as per advertisement in *Alta* and *Guide*.

(71)

www.ingramcontent.com/pod-product-compliance
Lightning Source LLC
Chambersburg PA
CBHW021530270326
41930CB00008B/1183